BECOMING A PRO

FOOTBALL PLAYER

BY RYAN NAGELHOUT

Gareth Stevens
PUBLISHING

Please visit our website, www.garethstevens.com. For a free color catalog of all our high-quality books, call toll free 1-800-542-2595 or fax 1-877-542-2596.

Library of Congress Cataloging-in-Publication Data

Nagelhout, Ryan.
Becoming a pro football player / by Ryan Nagelhout.
p. cm. — (Going pro)
Includes index.
ISBN 978-1-4824-2062-3 (pbk.)
ISBN 978-1-4824-2061-6 (6-pack)
ISBN 978-1-4824-2063-0 (library binding)
1. Football — Juvenile literature. 2. Football players — Juvenile literature. I. Nagelhout, Ryan. II. Title.
GV950.7 N34 2015
796.332—d23

First Edition

Published in 2015 by
Gareth Stevens Publishing
111 East 14th Street, Suite 349
New York, NY 10003

Copyright © 2015 Gareth Stevens Publishing

Designer: Nicholas Domiano
Editor: Therese Shea

Photo credits: Cover, p. 1 peepo/Vetta/Getty Images; p. 4 Photo Works/Shutterstock.com; p. 5 Doug Pensinger/Getty Images Sport/Getty Images; p. 7 (icons) Tanarch/Shutterstock.com; p. 7 (background) Mark Herreid/Shutterstock.com; p. 7 (field) Marius Antonescu/Shutterstock.com; p. 9 Robert Beck/Sports Illustrated/Getty Images; p. 10 Topical Press Agency/Hulton Archive/Getty Images; p. 11 Peter Weber/ Shutterstock.com; p. 13 Amy Myers/Shutterstock.com; p. 15 Larry St. Pierre/Shutterstock.com; p. 17 Jared Wickerham/Getty Images Sport/Getty Images; p. 19 Jeff Zelevansky/Getty Images Sport/Getty Images; p. 20 Harry How/Getty Images Sport/Getty Images; p. 21 Simon Bruty/Sports Illustrated/Getty Images; p. 23 Joe Robbins/Getty Images Sport/Getty Images; p. 25 Cliff Hawkins/Getty Images Sport/Getty Images; p. 27 Jonathan Daniel/Getty Images Sport/Getty Images; p. 28 James Flores/Getty Images Sport/ Getty Images; p. 29 Peter G. Aiken/Getty Images Sport/Getty Images.

Printed in the United States of America

CPSIA compliance information: Batch #CW15GS: For further information contact Gareth Stevens, New York, New York at 1-800-542-2595.

CONTENTS

Words in the glossary appear in **bold** type the first time they are used in the text.

THE PRO DREAM

Every **professional** football player grew up dreaming of winning the biggest game of all. In the National Football League (NFL), that game is called the Super Bowl. Just two teams can play in it each year, and only one can win.

You need to work hard for many years to play in the Super Bowl. From youth leagues to high school and college teams, players study hard and train to show they have what it takes to play this tough sport. Do you think you have the skills to beat the odds and make the NFL? Read on to learn more about becoming a professional football player!

SOCCER

AMERICAN FOOTBALL

The word "football" can be used to describe different sports all over the world. In the United States and Canada, football is the sport of quarterbacks and touchdowns. Outside of North America, football is what we call soccer. Australia also has its own version of football, called Australian Rules Football.

It takes many years of hard work—and some great talent—to make it to the NFL.

GETTING STARTED

Most pro football players follow the same basic path to the NFL. Players start learning to play on a team in youth football and then continue playing on a high school team. From there, they're **recruited** by colleges, where they play until they graduate or are **drafted** by a professional league.

Many pros began playing football when they were very young. They may have learned to throw and catch a football with a parent or friends. They practice running and kicking a football as well as learn the positions and rules of the game.

PICKING A POSITION

There are lots of different positions in football. People who throw the ball very well play quarterback. Those who run fast play wide receiver or running back. If you're very strong, you can play on the offensive or defensive line. Many people play both offense and defense growing up.

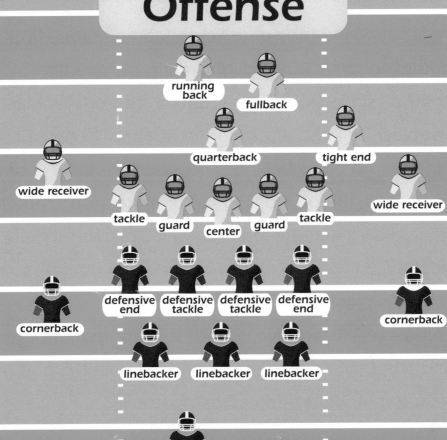

Offense

running back

fullback

quarterback

tight end

wide receiver

wide receiver

tackle

guard

center

guard

tackle

defensive end

defensive tackle

defensive tackle

defensive end

cornerback

cornerback

linebacker

linebacker

linebacker

free safety

strong safety

Defense

Different positions require different skills, so it's good to try as many as possible to find a good fit.

The next step is to play on a youth football team. Pop Warner football leagues have taught young players the game of football since 1929. Their leagues start at Tiny-Mite (5- to 7-year-olds) for kids who weigh from 35 to 75 pounds (16 to 34 kg) and go up to Unlimited leagues (11- to 14-year-olds) for kids who weigh 105 pounds (48 kg) or more. Pop Warner leagues feature both contact football, which allows tackling, and flag football, in which players remove flags from opponents instead of tackling them.

The Amateur Athletic Union (AAU) is a group that organizes football and other sports leagues across the United States. AAU leagues feature both flag and contact football.

A TOUGH SPORT

Any football player could get hurt on any play. Whether you're playing in youth leagues or with the pros, proper safety equipment, such as helmets and pads, is essential for preventing injury. It's also important for players to inform coaches and parents when they're hurt, especially head injuries.

USA Football is an organization that makes sure different leagues follow a similar set of rules.

LEARN TO PLAY

Youth football is the best way to learn how to play on a real football team. Every player must work with teammates on offense and defense. Players also learn how to do different drills that teach them to tackle and play their position better.

Football is a game in which the offense and defense run plays against one another. Learning how to run plays with your team is a big part of being good at football. Players sometimes get their own playbook, which contains all their team's plays. It's their job to study the playbook and practice so the plays work on the field.

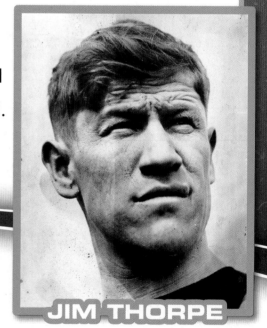

JIM THORPE

THORPE AND POP

Pop Warner football is named after Glenn Scobie "Pop" Warner, a football coach. Warner coached many great players, including Jim Thorpe, who is thought to be one of the greatest athletes of all time. Thorpe, a Native American, played football and lacrosse and won a gold medal in the **decathlon** in the 1912 Olympic Games.

The National Football League Players Association (NFLPA) says about 60 to 70 percent of all NFL players were on Pop Warner football teams.

SCHOOL AND FOOTBALL

After youth football, the next step for a future pro is usually to try out for a school's team. Many schools have **modified** football programs beginning in middle school. Students play in sixth, seventh, and eighth grades to get ready for high school football.

High school coaches often work with modified teams to get to know players and help them work on skills. They also teach players how to lift weights to get stronger.

In high school, teams are usually divided into varsity and junior varsity (JV) teams. The best players make the varsity, while the younger or less skilled athletes play JV football.

MAKING THE GRADE

It's important to study hard both on and off the football field. Knowing the playbook can help you play better. To stay on the team, though, you have to do well in school. Getting good grades in school will also help you get into a good college, so you can keep playing football while there!

Modified football leagues often use slightly different rules than high school football leagues.

GETTING RECRUITED

If you're a great high school player, people will take notice. Local newspapers may feature you in an article. College coaches and scouts will attend your games. They may talk to you about coming to their school to play football after you graduate. That means you're being recruited!

Playing football in college is the next stage to going pro. Some colleges offer athletic **scholarships** to play football there while attending classes. Many National Collegiate Athletic Association (NCAA) schools, such as the University of Alabama, have respected college football programs. Alabama is one of 125 NCAA **Division I** schools that play in the Football Bowl Subdivision (FBS).

AGE LIMITS

Almost all NFL players go to college to play football. This is because NFL teams can only draft players who are at least 3 years out of high school. Players picked in the NFL Draft have already finished their junior or senior season in college. They're usually drafted when they're about 21 years old.

You can track popular high school players during the recruiting process on websites such as rivals.com.

COLLEGE BALL

If you agree to play football at an NCAA school, you'll sign a National Letter of Intent that says you commit to playing there. Many players pick schools because of the coaching there, the school's location, or the promise of playing time.

Playing well in college shows NFL teams that you have what it takes to succeed against tougher competition. The game is faster, and players are more skilled than in high school. Athletes have to work even harder to keep up with other players at this level. Every team strives to win a championship, but playing well in any school conference can get you noticed.

RED SHIRTS

College athletes have 4 years of **eligibility** to play their sport. However, many are redshirted, or not allowed to play, their freshman year. This way, they can become more skilled through team practice and training for a year and keep their 4 years of eligibility of playing for the team.

NFL scouts—people who search for skilled athletes—start to take notice of strong players in college.

Getting time on the college field can be the difference in making it to the pros. The best way to make NFL teams notice you on a college team is to play well in especially important games. Successful NCAA teams get a lot of attention because they play televised games against rivals.

Some of the most popular teams play in the same conferences, such as the University of Alabama and the University of Auburn of the Southeastern Conference (SEC). College conference title games are often just as exciting as **bowl games** at the end of the season.

BIG REPUTATIONS

Playing at a respected college football school can get you noticed by NFL scouts. The University of Miami had one of their players picked in the first round of the NFL Draft each year from 1995 to 2008. That's 14 straight drafts with a player taken in the first 32 picks of the draft.

The Heisman Trophy is given to the best college football player every year, but not all Heisman winners find success in the pros.

OTHER ROUTES

If you aren't recruited by a major college, your pro dreams aren't finished. Joe Flacco played football at the University of Delaware, a Division I Football Championship Subdivision (FCS) program much smaller than the major FBS programs. But Flacco impressed scouts and was drafted eighteenth overall by the Baltimore Ravens in the 2008 NFL Draft. Flacco went on to lead the Ravens to a Super Bowl championship in 2013.

Division III college teams can produce NFL stars, too. Buffalo Bills star running back Fred Jackson went to Coe College of the Iowa Intercollegiate Athletic Conference before signing a contract with the Bills in 2006.

SWITCHING SPORTS

Not all NFL superstars focused on football in school. All-Pro tight end Antonio Gates played basketball in college at Kent State University before he signed as an undrafted **free agent** with the San Diego Chargers. Gates became one of the greatest tight ends in league history. He holds the Chargers all-time **reception** record.

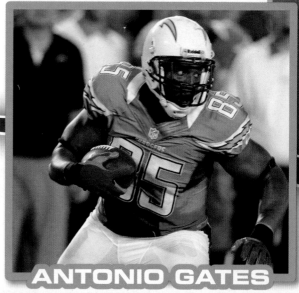

ANTONIO GATES

Joe Flacco won the Most Valuable Player award in Super Bowl XLVII.

THE COMBINE

One of the most important events for a football player is the NFL Combine, held each year several weeks before the draft. This event helps teams decide who to draft and in which order to draft them. Players are tested for intelligence, speed, strength, and their ability to do a number of football drills.

Colleges and universities may also hold their own "Pro Day" to which they invite NFL coaches, scouts, and reporters to watch their star players do a similar set of tests. The goal is to impress teams and improve "draft stock," or a player's chances of getting picked earlier in the draft.

LONG ODDS

About 9,000 people play college football every year, so making it to the NFL isn't easy. The National Football League Players Association reports that out of the 100,000 high school seniors who play football in the United States each year, only 215 ever make it to the NFL. That's just 0.2 percent!

A poor showing at the Combine or Pro Day can
hurt an athlete's chances of getting drafted.
About 300 players are invited to the NFL
Combine each year.

DRAFT DAY

The NFL Draft takes place over 3 days in New York City. All 32 NFL teams pick players over seven rounds, trying to build a championship team. After months and even years of scouting players, each team decides which players they want to join their team.

Players who think they'll be drafted may hire agents to help them sign contracts and handle the media attention. Many of the possible top draft players travel to New York to pose for photos and do interviews. Other players wait at home with their family. They hope for the telephone call that gives them the good news—they've been drafted!

OTHER OPTIONS

The NFL isn't the only professional football league in the world. Many college athletes who don't make the NFL play in the Canadian Football League (CFL), which has nine teams throughout Canada. Others play arena football or in semipro leagues throughout the United States. Many players spend time in both the CFL and NFL in their careers.

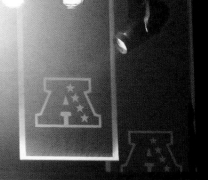

ROUND: 1
PICK: 23

ON THE CLOCK

6:09

PICK: 22

J. Manziel

QB

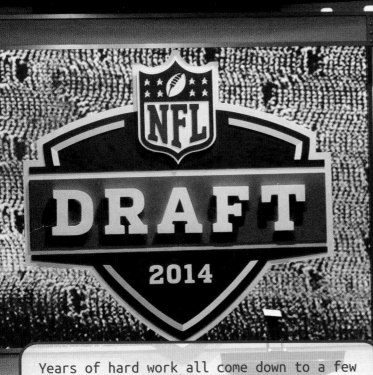

NFL DRAFT 2014

Years of hard work all come down to a few days in the spring.

WOMEN IN FOOTBALL

Lots of girls play youth football in Pop Warner leagues. Some even play in high school, usually as kickers or running backs. Holley Mangold played high school football in Ohio as a guard. Her brother, Nick, plays for the NFL's New York Jets.

Women also play in their own leagues such as the Women's Football Alliance. The first professional women's football league was the Women's Professional Football League, which ran from 1999 to 2007. The Independent Women's Football League started play in 2001 and currently has more than four dozen teams playing across the United States and Canada.

WOMEN GOING PRO

In 2014, Jen Welter became the first woman to carry the ball on a men's professional football team when she played for the Texas Revolution, an indoor football team. In 1970, Pat Parlinkas was a kick holder for the Orlando Panthers of the Continental Football League. Other women have been kickers for pro teams in the past.

Anyone can play football! Women have
played with men, but also have their own
pro football leagues in the United States
and Canada.

KEEP WORKING

Even after you're drafted, there's no promise of getting a spot on the team. Making an NFL **roster** is hard work. There can only be 53 players on a team to start the season. Draft picks go to training camps to get ready for league play and compete with other players for positions. Some draft picks taken in later rounds won't make the final cut.

There are about 1,700 players in all on the 32 teams in the NFL. If you become one of them, you can be proud of accomplishing what many young football players can only dream of!

SHORT CAREERS

George Blanda played 26 seasons in the NFL! Few players make it past 12 years in the league, though. Football is a tough sport, and the competition to make a team's roster is stiff. The average NFL career is 3½ seasons. Staying in the league is just as hard as making it!

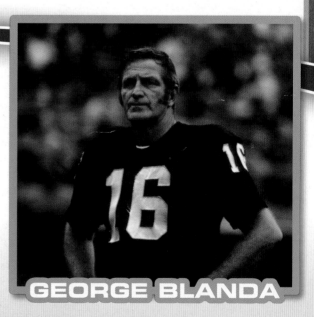

GEORGE BLANDA

There are no guaranteed contracts in the NFL, which means you always have to work hard to stay on the team.

GLOSSARY

bowl game: a postseason game played between champion or high-ranking college football teams

decathlon: an athletic contest made up of 10 events

Division I: the highest level of athletics in the National Collegiate Athletic Association (NCAA)

Division III: an NCAA group that consists of colleges that do not offer athletic scholarships

draft: to select a player from a pool of potential players entering a league. Also, the process of selecting new players.

eligibility: the amount of time a player is allowed to play in college

free agent: a player whose contract has ended, allowing them to sign a contract with a new team

modify: to make slight changes to something

professional: earning money from an activity that many people do for fun

reception: the catching of a pass made toward the opponent's goal

recruit: in sports, to persuade someone to be on a team

roster: a list of athletes on a team

scholarship: money awarded to a student to pay for their college education

FOR MORE INFORMATION

Books

Braun, Eric. *Super Football Infographics*. Minneapolis, MN: Lerner Publications, 2015.

Graves, Will. *The Best NFL Offenses of All Time*. Minneapolis, MN: ABDO Publishing, 2013.

Van Pelt, Don, and Brian Wingate. *An Insider's Guide to Football*. New York, NY: Rosen Central, 2015.

Websites

High School Football
maxpreps.com/national/football.htm
Search for information about high school football teams.

Official Site of the National Football League
nfl.com
Find schedules and more about the NFL.

Pro Football Reference
pro-football-reference.com
Visit this site to find statistics about your favorite players and teams.

INDEX